To:

Command (direct) it in your daily devotional time with God.

Minister Rich P. Successful

Date

Scan to Seed

1975 - ∞

DIVES

VALDE

FELIX

PROSPERUM

S

Fidem Remissionem Humilitas

This daily guide of devotionals has a little different twist than the usual. It gives us the opportunity to get our day started with a passage of scripture that is thought provoking and raises questions that searches the depths of our hearts. As a result should draw us closer to God, increase our spirituality and help us to live better days by following our own advice.

I hope we would take full advantage of the space provided to write our honest feelings in response to the questions posed. I thank God for using Minister Successful in providing us with this wonderful tool to bring us closer to a true spiritual awareness.

Those of us who begin their mornings with this devotional should emerge refreshed and connected to the Holy Spirit and each day should be better than the day before. For those who close their day with this devotional should rest easy knowing that the coming day is anchored in Christ.

Dr. Omer M. Reid, Pastor
Flagg Chapel Baptist Church

Dedication

I dedicate this book to my Kings (Rico Successful and Jehu Successful), my Queens (Mackenzie Successful and Alexandra Successful) and to my host of Aunts and Uncles. I would not be who God chose without your enduring love and unwavering patience.

Introduction:

Job 38:12-13
New King James Version (NKJV)

"Have you commanded the morning since your days began, And caused the dawn to know its place, That it might take hold of the ends of the earth, And the wicked be shaken out of it?

Through our daily devotion, we are to loose evil from its assignment over our mourning, day and night. We are to bind evil to its new assignment which is the footstool of Jesus. It is through our daily devotion that we destroy evil and its assignment against our day and our lives.

"Stop Looking At Things in the Natural"

EmPowerMent Scriptures:
1. Proverbs 3:5
New King James Version (NKJV)

Trust in the Lord with all your heart and lean not to your own understanding.

The Good News Translation

Trust in the Lord with all your heart and never rely on what you think you know.

2. Isaiah 55:8-9
New King James Version (NKJV)

For My thoughts are not your thoughts, nor are your ways My ways," says the Lord. For as the heavens are higher than the earth, so are My ways higher than your ways, And My thoughts than your thoughts.

With all the changes in the world you must trust in the Lord with all our heart. You cannot afford to be distracted by the natural (visible). It was Benjamin Franklin that said, "believe half of what you see and none of what you hear."

In the natural, both God and Noah looked like they were both out of their minds until it started raining on the earth for 40 days and 40 nights.

In the natural, why would God use Paul the murderer of the Christians to preach the gospel to the same Christians, he was responsible for putting in chains, beating and ultimately killing. In the natural, why would God tell Abraham and Sara long past the child-bearing age that they would have a child.

In the natural, why not come when Lazarus was sick and heal him? Why wait until he was dead for four days and raise him from the dead. In the natural, why not turn off the fiery furnace rather than allowing the fiery furnace to be turned up seven times on the three Hebrew boys. In the natural, why not expose Potiphar's wife as liar rather than allowing Joseph the dreamer to be disgraced.

In the natural, why not ease Pharaoh's heart to release the Children of Israel from slavery in Egypt rather than harden it. In the natural, why not allow Mary and Joseph to marry then get pregnant naturally instead of supernaturally with child and no man. God was teaching us and generations to come through each of these examples, that we serve a supernatural God and that there is nothing too hard for him if we stop looking at things in the natural.

1. What is God saying to you? How can you better prepare yourself to experience God's best? What are some ways you can stop looking at things in the natural? Why should you trust God more now than ever?

_____

_____

_____

_____

_____

_____

_____

_____

_____

_____

_____

_____

_____

_____

_____

_____

Let's Pray

Father God, I commit my heart to "fully" trust you with my day, in the mighty name of Jesus, Amen!

Be Strong in the Lord
and
The Supernatural Power of his might!!!

EmPowerMent Scripture:
1. Exodus 13:17-18
New Kings James Version (NKJV)

When Pharaoh let the people go, <u>God did not lead them</u> on the road through the Philistine country, though that was shorter for God said, "if they face war, they might change their minds and return to Egypt." 18 so God led the people <u>around by the desert</u> road toward the Red Sea.

We have all had to endure some type of challenge. At times, it can feel like God has abandoned you. Rest assured that God has not abandoned you. Like biblical Job, God is behind the scenes bringing you to the attention of the adversary. You may ask what made you a candidate to be brought to the attention of the adversary by God. It is your willingness to believe in the strength and supernatural power of God's might. God is in the soul winning business.

He is looking to recruit as many vessels that will believe and receive what Christ did on the cross. If you take inventory of your friends and associates are being challenged like you. God has not recommended any of them to the adversary because they are too weak. God knows they do not believe in his strength and supernatural power but through your testimony they will develop strength and power in God. I know your challenges look like they are working for your bad, don't be fooled. Each challenge has an ingredient of success and is working for your good.

2. How are your challenges working for your good? What are some ways that you can be strong in the Lord? How do you know God is a supernatural God? Why is soul winning so important to God?

_____

_____

_____

_____

_____

_____

_____

_____

_____

_____

_____

_____

_____

_____

_____

_____

_____

_____

_____

_____

_____

_____

_____

_____

_____

_____

_____

<u>Let's Pray</u>

Father God, you are a supernatural God, and my adversary is no match for you. I surrender the challenges of this day to you, in the mighty name of Jesus, Amen!

"Stay Connected"

EmPowerMent Scripture:
DANIEL 7:21-22
NEW KING JAMES VERSION

21 "I Daniel was watching; and the same horn was making war against the saints, and prevailing against them, verse. 22 until the ancient of days came, and a judgment was made in favor of the saints of the most high, and the time came for the saints to possess the kingdom.

The evil forces were prevailing against the saints because God's people didn't realize that they were not connected and yet under attack. It wasn't until the ancient of days came that they realized they were under attack. Who is the ancient of days? The ancient of days is God in you.

When you step forward, God steps forward. When you pray, God answers. When you seek, God provides. When you knock, God opens closed doors. You have been given a judgment in favor. This judgment in favor is our connection to God through prayer which was bought by the precious blood of lamb, Jesus Christ over 2,000 years ago.

I have heard it said, "the enemy is after your anointing." No that is incorrect theology. The enemy is after your connection with God. The anointing is no good if you are not connected to God, stay connected!

3. What are some ways you can stay connected? How can you improve your connection? How can you encourage someone else to stay connected?

_____

_____

_____

_____

_____

_____

_____

_____

_____

_____

_____

_____

_____

_____

_____

_____

_____

_____

_____

_____

<u>Let's Pray</u>

Father God, activate the power of the Ancient of Days over my day, in the mighty name of Jesus, Amen!

"What a difference a Mother can make!"

EmPowerMent Scripture:
Proverbs 13:22
NEW KING JAMES VERSION

A good man (blessed mother) leaves an inheritance to his (her) children's children.

As a real estate professional with over 2 decades of real estate experience, I became acquainted with a special Mother, due to her Pastor Son's decision to purchase his own church building. At the time, the contract was accepted he did not how he would finance the purchase of the building. All the banks that he met with said no! He knew, going back to Pastor his old church was not an option. He believed that God had greener pastures ahead for him and his ministry.

We were literally in a fixed fight, a "faith fight." It was right in the turbulence of the moment; God showed this Pastor exactly what to do next. Pastor made one phone call to Momma. He apprised his mother of the challenges, obstacles, and the need. Momma then called her oldest daughter; the oldest daughter called her youngest sister and the rest was history. The church was purchased with cash, no loan. One phone call to Momma changed the tide of the battle. One phone call to Momma changed everything in his favor.

4. Describe the difference your parents or parent-like figure has made in your life. What difference can you make in the life of someone else today? How can you be a positive role model in someone else's life like someone has been in your life?

_____

_____

_____

_____

_____

_____

_____

_____

_____

_____

_____

_____

_____

_____

_____

_____

_____

_____

Let's Pray

Father God, I stand on the shoulders of generations. Today, I ask you to help me to make a difference in someone else's life, in the mighty name of Jesus, Amen!

It is "Your" Time Now!!!

EmPowerMent Scripture:
Galatians 4:4
NEW KING JAMES VERSION

But when the fullness of the time had come, God sent forth his Son.

Like you, I have asked the Lord, why me and he answered why not you. He further, told me you have been built for the challenge, the battle, struggle, and opportunity. You have been built for the divorce, the sickness, and the grief. *It is Your Time Now!* God is calling you forward like he called the colt in Mark 11:1-2, that was all tied up. God is calling you forth into business; God is calling you forth into homeownership; God is calling you forth into marriage; God is calling you forth into ministry; God is calling you forth into healing; deliverance, peace, joy and happiness; God is calling you forth into that next level anointing; God is untying you because it is the fullness of his time.

5. What is God calling you forth into this next season of your life? What does this next season of your life look like? How has God prepared you for this next season? How do you know that it is your time now?

_____

_____

_____

_____

_____

_____

_____

_____

_____

_____

_____

_____

_____

_____

_____

_____

Let's Pray

Father God, I recognize that it is my time now. Father God, untie me from the hurt of yesterday, in the mighty name of Jesus, Amen!

"The Pain of Being Chosen"

EmPowerMent Scripture:
Luke 22:42
NEW KING JAMES VERSION

Jesus saying, "Father, if it is your will, take this cup away from me; nevertheless, not my will, but yours, be done.

If you are going to effectively become who God has ordained and predestine you to be, you must understand that God has a plan and purpose for your pain. It is your pain that gives God space to work and to operate his divine power in and through your life. It is your pain that God uses to impact the lives of the faithful and the faithless. It is your pain that God designed to impact and bless the entire world.

It is your pain that God designed to impact and bless generations born and unborn. Jesus knew that he was chosen to be pushed out of eternity into time and space. Jesus knew that God's purpose for pushing him out of eternity into time and space was greater than his pain.

Jesus knew he would have to endure not only the natural seasons of fall, winter, spring, and summer but Jesus also knew that he would have to endure the spiritual seasons of crucifixion, death, burial, and resurrection. Jesus knew the pain of being chosen.

6. What pain are you presently feeling in your life? Why do you feel that you are feeling this pain? Is this pain avoidable or necessary? What is your pain of being chosen?

_____

_____

_____

_____

_____

_____

_____

_____

_____

_____

_____

_____

_____

_____

_____

_____

<u>Let's Pray</u>

Father God, today I ask your help with the pain of being chosen, in the mighty name of Jesus, Amen!

"The Cost of Being Chosen"

EmPowerMent Scripture:
Acts 9:15-16
NEW KING JAMES VERSION

But the Lord said to him, go, for he is a chosen vessel of mine to bear my name before gentiles, kings, and the children of Israel. verse 16. For I will show him how many things he must suffer for my name's sake.

Saul encountered many of the same issues you are faced with today. Like Jesus, being chosen by God, newly converted Saul, had to endure the natural seasons of fall, winter, spring and summer. Additionally, Saul had to endure the spiritual seasons of crucifixion, death, burial, and resurrection. The first season is crucifixion (to be crucified is to be put to death by nailing or binding the hands and feet to a cross and being stabbed in the heart and left for dead). The second spiritual season is death (the irreversible separation of life functions). The third spiritual season is burial (the act of being buried). The final spiritual season is resurrection (restoration to life).

Like Jesus and Saul, you will have to endure the natural as well as the spiritual seasons of crucifixion (bound, stabbed in the heart and left for dead), death (permanent separation from those you knew you couldn't live without), burial (counted out, looked over, and buried alive) resurrection (restored back to life)

7. What spiritual season are you in? How do you know? What are you learning while you are in this spiritual season?

_____

_____

_____

_____

_____

_____

_____

_____

_____

_____

_____

_____

_____

_____

_____

_____

_____

<u>Let's Pray</u>

Father God, I ask your help in facing the spiritual seasons of this day, in the mighty name of Jesus, Amen!

"The Call of Being Chosen"

EmPowerMent Scripture:
I Samuel Chapter 3:7-11
NEW KING JAMES VERSION

Now Samuel did not yet know the Lord, neither was the word of the Lord yet revealed (released) unto him. verse 8. And the Lord called Samuel again the third time. So he arose and went to Eli, and said, "Here I am, for you did call me." Then Eli perceived that the Lord had called the boy. verse 9. Therefore, Eli said to Samuel, "Go, lie down; and it shall be, if he calls you, that you must say, 'Speak, Lord, for Your servant hears.'

I find it strange that God knew Samuel but Samuel did not know the Lord's voice. Samuel was a minister in training (MIT) and yet did not know the Lord's voice nor the revealed word of the Lord. What was the revealed word of the Lord? Samuel did not know that before he was formed in his mother's womb, that he had been consecrated, appointed, ordained, and chosen to be God's prophetic voice to the nations. There was a promise to God that was hanging over his life that had not been revealed to Samuel. The promise was, the spoken word of God out of his mother's (Hannah) mouth which committed him back to God.

Like Samuel, there is a call of God on your life. You have been chosen before the foundation of the world to be God's prophetic voice to the nations and the imaginations of the world.

8. What promise did your mother and father make to God concerning your life? What prophecies were spoken over your life as a child?

_____

_____

_____

_____

_____

_____

_____

_____

_____

_____

_____

_____

_____

_____

_____

_____

_____

Let's Pray

Father God, today I ask your help in hearing your voice this day Like Samuel cause my ear to be sensitive to your voice, in the mighty name of Jesus, Amen!

"Called to Conquer"

EmPowerMent Scripture:
Matthew Chapter 14:22-24
NEW KING JAMES VERSION

Immediately Jesus made his disciples get into the boat and go before him to the other side, while he sent the multitudes away. verse 23 When he sent the multitudes away. He went up on the mountain by himself to pray. Now when evening came, he was alone there. verse 24. But the boat was now in the middle of the sea, tossed by the waves for the wind was contrary.

We find Jesus's disciples getting into a boat, being sent into a storm, on their way to the other side. Why would God send his disciples into a storm? Let me rephrase that question, Why would God send you and I into a storm? Just like God knew the storm was nothing before his disciples. He also knows that the storm is nothing before us.

My question to you is, "What is it God knows about you that you have yet to discover about yourself?" What is it that your storm knows about you that you have yet to discover about yourself?

Let me answer that for you, you have been *called to conquer!!!*

9. What do you feel is God's purpose sending you into a storm? How does the storm help you to become a better witness for Jesus?

_____

_____

_____

_____

_____

_____

_____

_____

_____

_____

_____

_____

_____

_____

_____

_____

Let's Pray

Father God, I ask your help conquering these storms today, in the mighty name of Jesus, Amen!

"You are God's Masterpiece"

EmPowerMent Scripture:
Ephesians 2:10
NEW INTERNATIONAL VERSION

For we are God's masterpiece. He has created us anew in Christ Jesus, so we can do the good things (God things) he planned for us long ago.

You are an essential part of the institution we call church. As a member of your local church, you are a gift to your leaders and community. Your ministerial impact cannot be measured solely in financial tithing and offerings. God has no hands but your hands. God has no feet but your feet. God has no mouth but your mouth. It is your unselfish service and love for God through Jesus Christ, that draws others to ministry.

Although you are flawed you are still God's masterpiece. God is not looking for flawless servants but flawed. Apostle Paul was seeking to be flawless, and he asked God three times in the 2nd Book of Corinthians 12th Chapter 8th verse to remove his flaw, to remove the thorn from his flesh that he could become flawless. In verse 9, God refused him three times and said to Apostle Paul that his grace was sufficient. God was saying to Apostle Paul stay flawed because inside of Christ we are all flawless and inside the hand of God, "You are God's Masterpiece!"

10. Why does God call you a masterpiece? How does your flaws serve God's purpose?

_____

_____

_____

_____

_____

_____

_____

_____

_____

_____

_____

_____

_____

_____

_____

_____

_____

_____

_____

Let's Pray

Father God, I ask your help being your masterpiece today, in the mighty name of Jesus, Amen!

"You are Unstoppable"

EmPowerMent Scripture:
Matthew 14:29-30
NEW KING JAMES VERSION

So he said, "Come." And when Peter had come down out of the boat he walked on the water to go to Jesus. verse 30 But when he saw that the wind was boisterous, he was afraid; and beginning to sink he cried out, saying "Lord, save me!"

God is looking for someone that is willing to ignore the wind and walk on water, walk in the realm of blessing, impossibility, healing, deliverance, joy, happiness, peace, prosperity, wealth, success, miracles, signs, and wonders.

God is looking for someone that he can trust with trouble, he can trust with a failed marriage, he can trust with a failed business, a broken relationship, a failed educational system, a failed financial system, a failed political system, a failed government and economy, a failed child-care system, a failed ministry, a failed community, and a failed nation. You are that person, keep your eyes on Jesus and keep walking....

11. What impossible situation has God called you to walk on? How has God prepared you to walk on this impossible situation?

_____

_____

_____

_____

_____

_____

_____

_____

_____

_____

_____

_____

_____

_____

_____

_____

_____

_____

_____

_____

_____

Let's Pray

Father God, I thank you for trusting me with impossibility. I am asking your help this day, in the mighty name of Jesus, Amen!

"You are Unbreakable"

EmPowerMent Scripture:
I Kings 18:41-44
NEW KING JAMES VERSION

Then Elijah said to Ahab, "Go up, eat and drink; for there is the sound of abundance of rain." So Ahab went up to eat anddrink. And Elijah went up to the top of Carmel; then he bowed down on the ground, and put his face between his knees, (he took up a prayer). And said to his servant, "Go up now, look toward the sea." So he went up and looked, and said, "There is nothing." And seven times he said, "Go again." Then it came to pass the seventh time, that he said, "There is a cloud, as small as a man's hand, rising out of the sea!" So he said, "Go up, say to Ahab, 'Prepare your chariot, and go down before the rain stops you.'

The Prophet Elijah began to pray, and he prayed 6 times and no sign of rain, there was no sign of deliverance, no sign of breakthrough, no sign of change in his circumstances. But the Prophet did not give up. The Prophet knew that he was *unbreakable*. What was the Prophet's response to what he did not see?

The Prophet's response was more prayer, and the bible says on the seventh time he prayed it came to pass. The situation you are facing right now did not come to stay it has come to pass. Don't give up, keep praying, you are about to hear and see the abundance of change (rain).

12. What are you believing God for? What should be your response when you feel God has not answered your prayers?

_____

_____

_____

_____

_____

_____

_____

_____

_____

_____

_____

_____

_____

_____

_____

_____

<u>Let's Pray</u>

Father God, I ask you to increase my diligence to remain prayerful this day, in the mighty name of Jesus, Amen!

"You are Unshakeable"

EmPowerMent Scripture:
Ruth 1:14
NEW KING JAMES VERSION

Then they lifted up their voices and wept again; and Orpah kissed her mother-in-law, but Ruth clung to her.

Ruth lost her husband, the love of her life, and her brother-in-love to the hands of untimely death. Without question, Ruth had hopes of starting her own family one day. She had high hopes, dreams and aspirations that were all cut short. Like you, your high-hopes, dreams, and aspirations have been cut short. Possibly, at no fault of your own or maybe cut short because of something you did.

Nevertheless, the scripture tells us that in the face of Ruth's enormous pain and tragedy, she clung to Naomi (her mother-in-love). Ruth was *unshakeable*.

Like Ruth, in the face of our enormous pain, adversity and disappointment, we must cling to Jesus. Despite it all we must remain, *unshakeable*.

13. What does unshakeable mean to you? What can you learn and incorporate in your life from Ruth's story?

_____

_____

_____

_____

_____

_____

_____

_____

_____

_____

_____

_____

_____

_____

_____

_____

_____

_____

_____

_____

_____

_____

_____

Let's Pray

Father God, like Ruth, I cling to you this day. in the mighty name of Jesus, Amen!

"You are Destined for Greatness"

EmPowerMent Scripture:
I Samuel 16:11
NEW KING JAMES VERSION

And Samuel said to Jesse, "Are all the young men here?" Then he said, "There remains yet the youngest (the forgotten), and there he is, keeping the sheep." And Samuel said to Jesse, "send and bring him. For we will not sit down till he comes here."

David was over-looked, looked down upon, and was not invited to the selection party at his own house. David was still destined for greatness. The stature of David's brothers nor the partiality of his parents, could stop or alter God's plan for his life.

Like David, you are not hard to find. Whether you are on social media or not. God knows where you are. Don't worry about being forgotten, promotion, and elevation will find you.

14. How are you being overlooked? Do you see God's plan at work amid your present circumstances? How does this story about David inspire you to believe in God's plan for your life?

_____

_____

_____

_____

_____

_____

_____

_____

_____

_____

_____

_____

_____

_____

_____

_____

_____

_____

_____

_____

_____

_____

_____

_____

<u>Let's Pray</u>

Father God, I ask this day, that you cause promotion and elevation to find me, in the mighty name of Jesus, Amen!

"You are Untouchable"

EmPowerMent Scripture:
Exodus 25:14; I Samuel 6:6
NEW KING JAMES VERSION

Exodus 25:14; You shall put the poles into the rings on the side of the ark, that the ark may be carried by them.

Second Samuel 6: 6; Uzzah put out his hand to the ark of God and took of it, for the oxen stumbled. Then the anger of the Lord was aroused against Uzzah, and God struck him there for his error; and he died there by the ark of God.

Scripture teaches us that the Ark of God's covenant was not to be mishandled. God had specific instructions in how the ark was to be carried. In the same manner, God has specific instructions on how you are to be handled. You are not to be handled carelessly.

Here are a few of God's instructions; God said in Genesis Chapter 12 verse 3, whoever curses (mishandles) you shall be cursed and whoever blesses you shall be blessed. This was the covenant made to us through Abraham; therefore, if someone comes to bless you they can expect a blessing. If someone comes to curse (mishandle) you, they can expect a curse.

In Psalms Chapter 105, verse 15, God says touch (mishandle) not my anointed ones and do my prophets any harm. Do you wonder why? It's because through the word of God you are *untouchable*. The lies, the shame, the heartache, and the pain were the cost to another level, another dimension in God. What level, what dimension, *"untouchable!"*

15. How has God's word made you untouchable? What are some instances that you feel God has made you untouchable?

_____
_____
_____
_____
_____
_____
_____
_____
_____
_____
_____
_____
_____
_____

Let's Pray

Father God, I ask your help this day to stand on your word, in the mighty name of Jesus, Amen!

"You are Unforgettable"

EmPowerMent Scripture:
Isaiah 49:16
NEW KING JAMES VERSION

Behold, I have engraved thee upon the palms of my hands; your walls are ever before me.

The Prophet Isaiah, said that God has engraved, meaning he has tattooed, your name in the palm of his hands, you are *unforgettable*. God has intentionally fixed you in his divine mind, plan, and hand of protection. He has engraved and tatted you, and everyone that is connected to you, associated with you and related to you in his presence, power, plan, protection and his mind. The song writer said, "he has the whole wide world in his hands, meaning his mind."

The Prophet Isaiah, in the b-part of our scripture, says that our walls are continually before the Lord. This prophetic word from Prophet Isaiah was to comfort Israel. The Prophet was letting Israel know that they were *unforgettable*, they were commemorated and memorialized in the mind of God, continually.

Like, the Prophet Isaiah, I come to comfort you. This is not how your story end. It's simply where your story has taken a turn you didn't expect. God is never late he is always right on time. Don't dwell on unanswered questions, or unsolved problems or unequipped battles. Your unanswered question, problem or hardship doesn't have the final say. God has the final say and God says, "you are *unforgettable!!!*

16. Does it matter that God has engraved your name in the palm of his hands? What does this mean to you? How does this fact encourage you to seize the day?

_____

_____

_____

_____

_____

_____

_____

_____

_____

_____

_____

_____

_____

_____

_____

Let's Pray

Father God, I ask you to guide me this day, in the mighty name of Jesus, Amen!

"Fear Nothing"

EmPowerMent Scripture:
John 5:5-8
NEW KING JAMES VERSION

Now a certain man was there who had an infirmity thirty- eight years. When Jesus saw him lying there, and knew that he already had been in that condition a long time, He said to him, "Do you want to be made well?" The sick man answered Him, "Sir, I have no man to put me into the pool when the water is stirred up; but while I am coming, another steps down before me." Jesus said to him, "Rise, take up your bed and walk."

Our Jesus, the lily in the valley, the bright and morning star, tells the man sitting at the pool of Bethesda for 38 years, it is time, to take up thy bed and walk. Like Jesus, I have been sent to tell you that it is your time to take up your bed and walk. It is time to take up your deliverance and walk. It is time to take up your healing and walk. It is time to take up your excuses, your joy, peace, and happiness and walk.

You are in the world to win the world not by fear but by your faith in God. Your iphone light should not be more recognizable than your life. Your life should shine visibly, that others will come out of their darkness, wickedness and begin to shine... in faith not fear. The cemetery is where dreams die, the sanctuary is where new dreams are born and where dead dreams can live again.

Fear nothing, because there is no limits to what your God can do, what he has done for others he will do the same for you.

17. What's limiting your progress? What steps can you take in faith that will allow you to overcome your fears?

_____

_____

_____

_____

_____

_____

_____

_____

_____

_____

_____

_____

_____

_____

<u>Let's Pray</u>

Father God, I desire to fear nothing. I ask your help this day to prevail in faith over fear, in the mighty name of Jesus, Amen!

"Together We Stand"

EmPowerMent Scripture:
Zechariah 12:8
NEW KING JAMES VERSION

In that day the LORD will defend the inhabitants of Jerusalem; the one who is feeble among them in that day shall be like David, and the house of David shall be like God,

God was promising us through Zechariah, a day when he would supernaturally empower his people. God has sent me to you mystical Jerusalem as your modern-day Zechariah, to let you know that he has a plan. When speaking that in that day, it means in this day, you will be like David, but *together we stand.* You will be as the House of David and corporately like God. As a corporate body who above hell, below hell and in hell would like to mess with God's children.

This is God's plan, *together we stand.* It activates God's defense, offense, mercy, vengeance, and justice for the inhabitants of the church, community, nation and foremost his people.

Sometimes God will place you in a distinct disadvantage that you can learn your advantage.

18. What is your advantage that God is trying to show you? How can you activate God's supernatural power in your situation? What is the benefit of standing together with others?

_____

_____

_____

_____

_____

_____

_____

_____

_____

_____

_____

_____

_____

_____

_____

_____

_____

_____

<u>Let's Pray</u>

Father God, I ask you to supernaturally empower me for this day, in the mighty name of Jesus, Amen!

"This is Your Performance Season"

EmPowerMent Scripture:
Luke 1:45
NEW KING JAMES VERSION

Blessed is she/he who believe for there will be a fulfillment of those things which were told her/him from the Lord.

You are not only in the natural seasons of fall, winter, spring, summer, but you are in your performance season. In your performance season you can expect God to perform that which he has spoken in and over your life.

Your performance season is not designed to take you out but to take you in. Your performance season is not designed to take you out but to take you up and over. God can only do for you, what you believe he can. God's performance is only limited by the size of your faith. Big faith in God produces big performance from God. Little faith in God produces little performance in God.

Dare to believe this is your performance season. Watch God perform signs, wonders, miracles, and blessings too numerous to count, too big to measure.

19. What have you learned about your performance season? How can you increase the size of God's performance in your performance season?

_____

_____

_____

_____

_____

_____

_____

_____

_____

_____

_____

_____

_____

_____

_____

_____

_____

_____

_____

_____

_____

_____

Let's Pray

Father God, I dare to believe this is my performance season, in the mighty name of Jesus, Amen!

"It's a Changing of the Guard"

EmPowerMent Scripture:
1 Corithians 16:13
NEW INTERNATIONAL VERSION

Be on guard; stand firm in the faith; be courageous, be strong.

In the natural, a changing of the guard or changes of the guard refers to a ceremony during which soldiers or other officials guarding a major government building or residence for example, Buckingham Palace in England are replaced by a new shift.

In a spiritual sense, a lot of these funerals in the Covid-19 era were ceremonies during which soldiers or other officials charged with guarding the gospel were replaced through transition. This transition was in favor of change which required new ministerial leaders with new training, fresh insight, strategies, tactics, and plans from God. These leaders have been further equipped and empowered to fight and win, the ongoing battle of soul winning in this New Millennium.

It is this Millennial generation that is learning about God outside the traditional four walls of the church. This generation is learning about God from platforms like Instagram, Facebook, Twitter, Tik Tok, Snap Chat and You-Tube. The old tactics of soul winning is no longer palatable. Most times change is received with a closed fist instead of an open hand.

Most churches were not ready to win these souls because some churches did not know technology or even how to spell technology. Covid-19 did not close any church. It was the lack of foresight and fear of change that closed many of the churches in this era.

20. How can you best prepare yourself for future changes in your life? How can you best prepare for future changes in your business and/or ministry?

_____

_____

_____

_____

_____

_____

_____

_____

_____

_____

_____

_____

_____

_____

_____

<u>Let's Pray</u>

Father God, I ask you to prepare me today for the changes that awaits tomorrow, in the mighty name of Jesus, Amen!

"It's a Setup"

EmPowerMent Scripture:
Daniel 2:21
KING JAMES VERSION

And he changeth the times and the seasons: he removeth kings, and setteth up kings: he giveth wisdom unto the wise, and knowledge to them that know understanding.

God setup Job to be afflicted. God setup Joseph to be betrayed. God setup Jacob to trick Isaac. God setup Moses to kill the Egyptian. God setup Pharaoh's heart to be harden. God setup Sara to laugh. God setup Hagar to be entangled. God setup Zacharias to be silenced. God setup the Prophet Hosea to marry a harlot.

God setup Mephibosheth to be dropped. God setup Leah to be hated. God setup Hannah to be barren. God setup David to battle Goliath. God setup himself to be sold out as Jesus the Christ.

God is demonstrating through each of these examples, the afflictions, betrayals, harden hearts, tricks, being laughed at, an entanglement, a bad marriage, bad health, being barren, the battles of life and being sold out are not to be considered as setbacks but setups.

You have been setup for the dynamic and redemptive power of God to be revealed through your life.

21. What setbacks have you encountered? How do you feel these setbacks have prepared you for God's setup?

_____

_____

_____

_____

_____

_____

_____

_____

_____

_____

_____

_____

_____

_____

_____

_____

_____

_____

Let's Pray

Father God, I ask for your help to see beyond my setbacks, in the mighty name of Jesus, Amen!

"Hope Again"

EmPowerMent Scripture:
Genesis 26:18
NEW KING JAMES VERSION

And Isaac dug again the wells of water which they had dug in the days of Abraham his father, for the Philistines had stopped them up after the death of Abraham. He called them by the names which his father had called them.

Isaac had been charged with the enormous task of digging the wells of his father, in search of water. These wells had been filled with dirt (jealousy, envy, contention, strive, misunderstandings, lies, betrayal, and false accusations) but Isaac didn't give up.

Like Isaac, you will have enemies in your path and on your path. You might feel stuck, defeated, hopeless and can't see your way. It is in these moments you must hope again. Isaac continued hope again and ultimately he found water.

22. What dream have you given up on? What lesson did you learn from Isaac?

_____

_____

_____

_____

_____

_____

_____

_____

_____

_____

_____

_____

_____

_____

_____

_____

_____

_____

_____

_____

_____

_____

_____

_____

Let's Pray

Father God, I ask your help to hope again, in the mighty name of Jesus, Amen!

"There is Strength in your Wilderness"

EmPowerMent Scripture:
2 Corinthians 12:9
NEW KING JAMES VERSION

And He said to me, "my grace is sufficient for you, for my strength is made perfect in weakness." Therefore most gladly I will rather boast in my infirmities, that the power of Christ may rest upon me.

The greatest enemy you must train to fight against is self-dependency. It is in the wilderness that you learn how and why you must depend solely on God. Everything you will ever need is never outside of God. Everyone and everything you need beckons to the voice of God. God is never concerned about how quick you arrive in your blessing field. God is most concerned about you arriving in your wilderness.

God knows with proper training in the wilderness you will be able to last in his blessing field. God's strength is always made perfect in your wilderness.

23. How has your wilderness experience strengthened you? What lessons have you learned in the wilderness that has prepared you for God's blessing field?

_____

_____

_____

_____

_____

_____

_____

_____

_____

_____

_____

_____

_____

_____

_____

_____

_____

_____

_____

_____

_____

_____

_____

_____

Let's Pray

Father God, I ask for wilderness strength this day, in the mighty name of Jesus, Amen!

"The Lion of Judah is my weapon"

EmPowerMent Scripture:
2 Corinthians 10:4
NEW KING JAMES VERSION

For the weapons of our warfare are not carnal but mighty in God for pulling down strongholds, casting down arguments and every high thing that exalts itself against the knowledge of God, bringing every thought into captivity to the obedience ofChrist.

Child of God, your guns, gun laws, police, military, Congress, and Constitution has no effect on evil forces. A classic example of an evil force and our vulnerability was Covid- 19.

Your gun, gun laws, police, military, Congress, and Constitution had no effect against this evil force. Be encouraged light shines brightest in darkness.

The darkness simply creates a demand not for Senators, Congressmen, Legislators, and Judicial Appointees but for you a child God. The demand is for you to come forth not just to speak the mind of God but to be the mind of God in the earth (your workplace, your home, and your church).

How is it a herd of lions led by a sheep lose to a herd of sheep led by a lion? It's called leadership. Jesus is your lion. He is the Lion of Judah, your leader and mighty weapon.

24. Why doesn't our gun laws work against evil forces? Why is the Lion of Judah so effective against evil forces? How can you properly use the Lion of Judah as your weapon against evil forces?

_____

_____

_____

_____

_____

_____

_____

_____

_____

_____

_____

_____

_____

_____

_____

_____

_____

_____

<u>Let's Pray</u>

Father God, I ask you to protect me this day, in the mighty name of Jesus, Amen!

"Hear Faith"

EmPowerMent Scripture:
Romans 10:17
NEW KING JAMES VERSION

So, then faith comes by hearing and hearing the word of God.

Christian congregants are in a crisis. Yet in every crisis there is both a danger and opportunity. You were never supposed to follow the man or woman of God, solely. You were supposed to follow them as they follow Christ. I believe there is a shift coming to the body of Christ, that will redirect congregants back to Christ.

This shift will cause the masses to follow Christ, the man or woman of God follows. In these coming days, less faith will be placed in leaders and more faith will be placed on Christ. The true leader of our faith, who these leaders follow. The enemy is running rapid to turn people away from hearing faith in God. It is this faith that produces action and change in the heart of people.

The scandals, and rumors being heard around the world are all distractions that will shift congregants back to a Christ centered faith, in God.

25. Why is hearing from God so important to your faith? Why is the shift back to a Christ centered faith necessary?

_____

_____

_____

_____

_____

_____

_____

_____

_____

_____

_____

_____

_____

_____

_____

_____

_____

_____

_____

_____

_____

_____

<u>Let's Pray</u>

Father God, help me to hear your words of faith over my day, in the mighty name of Jesus, Amen!

"Even More"

EmPowerMent Scripture:
2 Samuel 12:7-8
NEW KING JAMES VERSION

I anointed you king over Israel, and I delivered you from the hand of Saul. I gave your master's house to you, and your master's wives into your arms. I gave you the house of Israel and Judah. And if all this had been too little, I would have given you even more. Why did you despise the word of the LORD by doing what is evil in his eyes?

God sends the Prophet Nathan to King David to let him know that he did not have to commit adultery or murder. All he had to do was ask. God was letting King David know, that he was standing ready to do even more for him.

Like Prophet Nathan, God has sent me to inform you that he is willing to do even more for you as well. There is no reason for you to settle or backslide, commit adultery, fornication, murder, or lie in wait. God is standing ready and willing to do even more, you simply must ask.

26. What have you learned from King David's mistake? Why is it so easy for us to settle and/or compromise? Do you see God as being able to do even more? What changes are you willing to make to receive even more from God?

_____

_____

_____

_____

_____

_____

_____

_____

_____

_____

_____

_____

_____

_____

_____

_____

_____

<u>Let's Pray</u>

Father God, I am believing you for even more today, in the mighty name of Jesus, Amen!

"Armloads of Blessings"

EmPowerMent Scripture:
Pslams 126:6
MESSAGE BIBLE

So those who went off with heavy hearts will come home laughing, with armloads of. blessing.

The pain, disappointment, sorrow, guilt is all confirmation that God has something better or even someone better ahead for you. Your responsibility is to stop mismanaging and rehearsing the pain, the trauma, difficulty, and hardship.

Get past your pain and trust God to connect the dots. The pain was never designed to kill you, but it was designed to build you. The greater the arms of trouble, tribulations, and problems the greater the *armloads of blessings*.

27. Why are you rehearsing your pain? What is the correlation between your arms of trouble and the armloads of blessing God has for you?

_____

_____

_____

_____

_____

_____

_____

_____

_____

_____

_____

_____

_____

_____

_____

_____

_____

_____

_____

_____

_____

_____

_____

_____

<u>Let's Pray</u>

Father God, I pray for my armloads of blessings to be released this day, in the mighty name of Jesus!

"You are Healed"

EmPowerMent Scripture:
Pslams 107:20
NEW KING JAMES VERSION

He sent His word and healed them, And delivered them from their destructions.

I believe your healing and deliverance is in the word of God. Often, we seek comfort from friends and assistance from everyone else but God. If you took inventory over your life how would things look if you received God's word? How would things look if you accepted the comfort God's word provides? How would things look if you accepted the deliverance his word provides?

The Psalmist found that the sent word of God contained healing and deliverance. He found that like an ointment the sent word of God could be applied to any situation, and it would heal and deliver.

28. Do you believe that there is healing and deliverance in the word of God? What situation are you dealing with that could use the healing and deliverance power of the word of God? How should the word of God be applied in that situation?

_____

_____

_____

_____

_____

_____

_____

_____

_____

_____

_____

_____

_____

_____

_____

_____

_____

_____

<u>Let's Pray</u>

Father God, I pray for healing and deliverance over my day, in the mighty name of Jesus!

"Magnify the Lord"

EmPowerMent Scripture:
PSALM 34:3-5
KING JAMES VERSION

O magnify the LORD with me, And let us exalt his name together. I sought the LORD, and he heard me, And delivered me from all my fears. They looked unto him, and were lightened: And their faces were not ashamed.

Your problems and situations all seek to be placed in the forefront of your mind. It can appear like a race to depress and overwhelm you. Nevertheless, you must run even faster to magnify the Lord over and in your problems. You must run even faster against the anxiety of your adversary. How do you magnify the Lord, you may ask?

You magnify the Lord with scripture that places the Lord in front of your problems. You magnify the Lord with scripture that exalts the Lord over your problems. You magnify the Lord with scripture that encourages faith over fear.

29. What are some more scripture-based ways and strategies that you can use to magnify the Lord? How will these strategies help you in the future?

_____

_____

_____

_____

_____

_____

_____

_____

_____

_____

_____

_____

_____

_____

_____

_____

_____

_____

Let's Pray

Father God, be magnified over my day, in the mighty name of Jesus, Amen!

"A Greater Assignment"

EmPowerMent Scripture:
1 CORINTHIANS 7:17
EASTERN STANDARD VERSION

Only let each person lead the life that the Lord has assigned to him, and to which God has called him.

We are learning that drugs do not cure diseases they just change the former location of the disease. We are learning that age is not affecting your memory but the mercury filings and other metals in your mouth, cholesterol lowering medication and a fat free diet is affecting your memory.

According to John Hopkins more than 250,000.00 people in America are killed because of doctor mistakes. These mistakes are the 3 rd leading cause of death in America behind heart disease and cancer.

Abroad the dollar may have lost its value, but the Kingdom of God is increasing in value. What are you saying Minister Rich? What I am saying is that God's assignment on your life is greater than heart disease, cancer, doctor mistakes and even the enemy's assignment against your life.

My question to you is, what is it the enemy knows about you that you have yet to discover about yourself? The enemy knows that you have a greater assignment on your life to which God has called you.

30. What do you feel is the greater assignment that God has on your life? How do you know that this is your assignment? How will you pursue fulfilling this assignment?

Let's Pray

Father God, I accept the greater assignment on my life today, in the mighty name of Jesus, Amen!

"Sell Out"

EmPowerMent Scripture:
ISAIAH 40:8
NEW KING JAMES VERSION

The grass withers, the flower fades, But the word of our God stands forever.
The more you believe the word of God the more you will see God move on and in your behalf. The word of God promises that God will bring everything and everyone you need to pass in the fulfillment of your life. This is why you are not desperate, but you are blessed. You are not defeated, but you are rewarded. You are not disappointed, but you are renewed.

You are not lacking, but you are restored. You are not a democrat, republican or independent but you are a child of God. You are not black, or white but you are red covered by the precious blood of Jesus.

Your destiny and blessings are determined by the word of God. Abundant life requires abundant belief in the word of God. The word of God has made you victorious. The word of God has made you rich, prosperous, and successful in every area of your life. If God has richly blessed you like he has, imagine how much more he will do, when you sell out.

31. What does sell out to God mean to you? What changes should you make? Why should those changes be made? How should you make those changes? When should you make those changes? Why should you make those changes?

_____

_____

_____

_____

_____

_____

_____

_____

_____

_____

_____

_____

_____

_____

_____

_____

_____

Let's Pray

Father God, I desire to sell out to your word, your will, and your way, in the mighty name of Jesus, Amen!

Send Testimonials:
Email: RichPSuccessful@gmail.com

www.ingramcontent.com/pod-product-compliance
Lightning Source LLC
Chambersburg PA
CBHW041429120626
46547CB00002B/150